SCHOLASTIC

KITTY
Preschool
ACTIVITY BOOK

Editor: Ourania Papacharalambous
Cover design: Tannaz Fassihi
Cover art: Jen Naalchigar
Interior design: Jenny Rez
Interior images: © Shutterstock.com

ISBN 978-1-338-73872-8

3 4 5 6 7 8 9 10   40   26 25 24 23 22

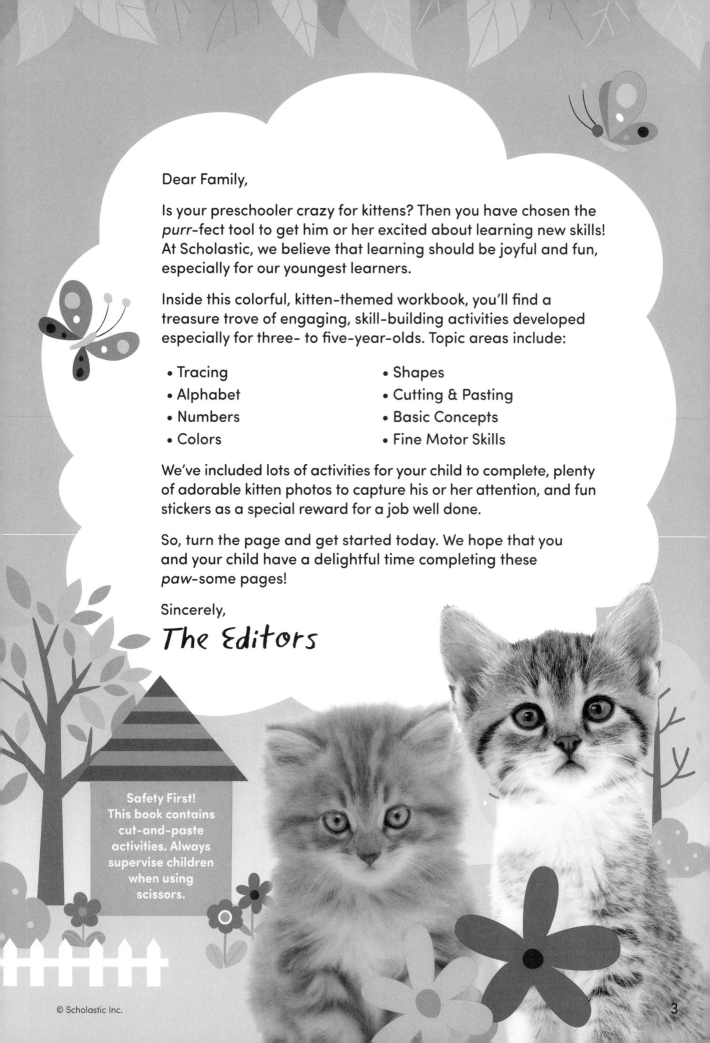

Dear Family,

Is your preschooler crazy for kittens? Then you have chosen the *purr*-fect tool to get him or her excited about learning new skills! At Scholastic, we believe that learning should be joyful and fun, especially for our youngest learners.

Inside this colorful, kitten-themed workbook, you'll find a treasure trove of engaging, skill-building activities developed especially for three- to five-year-olds. Topic areas include:

- Tracing
- Alphabet
- Numbers
- Colors

- Shapes
- Cutting & Pasting
- Basic Concepts
- Fine Motor Skills

We've included lots of activities for your child to complete, plenty of adorable kitten photos to capture his or her attention, and fun stickers as a special reward for a job well done.

So, turn the page and get started today. We hope that you and your child have a delightful time completing these *paw*-some pages!

Sincerely,

The Editors

Safety First! This book contains cut-and-paste activities. Always supervise children when using scissors.

Trace the lines from each kitten to its mother.

© Scholastic Inc.

Trace the lines to each kitten's bed.

Trace the lines to each kitten's toy.

Kitty Preschool Activity Book

Trace the lines to each kitten's scratching post.

Trace the armchair.

Trace each kitty. Then color the picture.

Aa

Adopt

Trace.

Adopt

Write.

A

a

Color the pictures that begin with A.

Bb

Bed

Trace.

Bed

Write.

B

b

 ____ all ____ ox

Help the kitten find its food.

Draw a line from each kitten to its mother.

|

Trace.

Write.

Circle each **I**.

2   3   3   2   3   2   I

     3   2   2   2   3

I   3   I   3   3   3

3   2   3   2   3

3   I   I   2   I   2   2

Find each I. Color that space ![ORANGE] .
Then color the rest of the picture.

Draw a bed for the kitten's friend.

Cut out the puzzle pieces. Use them to make a kitten! Paste the pieces in the frame.

Circle **5** differences.

Cc

Cat

Trace.

Cat

Write.

C

c

Circle **C** and **c**.

b	B	c	g	c	Q	P
p	p	C	D	b	G	g
C	G	Q	B	B	G	C
c	P	B	g	c	d g	c

Dd

Dish

Trace.

Write.

D

d

Circle the toys with the letters **D** and **d**.

Red

Circle the things that are red.

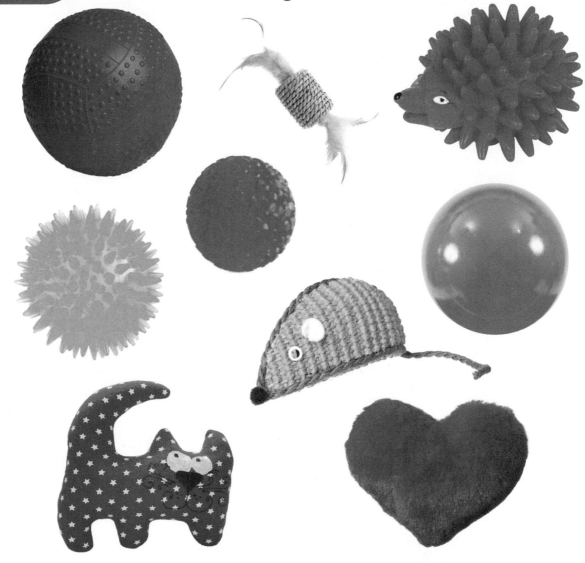

Color the toy mouse  RED .

Circle the cat that is **big** in each set.

2

Trace.

Write.

Draw **2** balls for the kitten to play with.

Circle the things that come in 2's.

Color the picture. Use the color key.

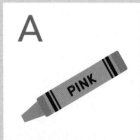

A PINK

B BLUE

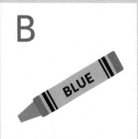

C ORANGE

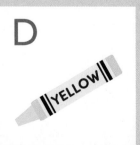

D YELLOW

Cut out the lowercase letters. Paste each next to its matching uppercase letter.

A

B

C

D

Trace the circle and the square.

square   circle

Color the circles **blue**. Color the squares **orange**.

E e

Ear

Trace.

Ear

Write.

Trace the kitty's ear. Write **e** on the ear. Then color the picture.

Ff

Fur

Trace.

Fur

Write.

2 →
1
3 →

F

1
2 →

f

Color the shapes with the letters **F** and **f**.

Help the kitten find the toy mouse.

Circle the picture that is **different** in each set.

3

3

Trace.

Write.

Color the shapes with the number 3.

Draw **3** toys for the kitten to play with.

Count the kittens. Write the number.

Cut out the pictures. Paste the correct number of cats in each space below.

1	2	3

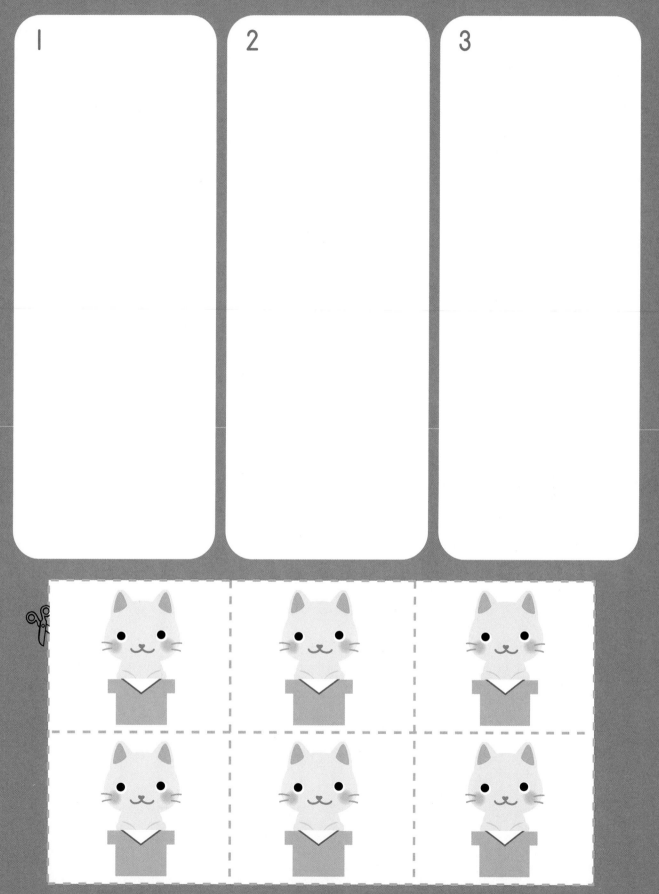

Circle **5** differences.

Gg

Goldfish

Trace.

Write.

Write **g** on each bowl.

Hh

Hat

Trace.

Write.

H

h

t   t   f   h   f   f   H   f   b   t   b   h

f   H   b   T   f   b   H   B   f

H   b   T   f   f   T   h   B   b   b   t

F   F   t   f   T   B   b   t

Circle the things that are yellow.

Color the kitten's bowl  YELLOW .

What comes next? Draw it!

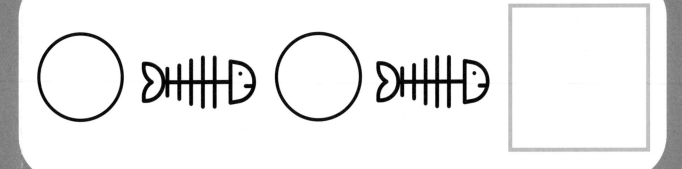

4

4

Trace.

Write.

Color 4 stars on the kitten's bed.

Draw **4** stripes on the kitten.

Connect each kitten to the toy with the matching uppercase letter.

Cut out the kittens. Paste them in order of age from youngest to oldest.

youngest to oldest

Find and circle these items in the big picture.

In

Trace.

In

Write.

i

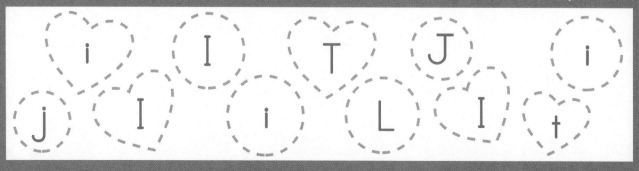

J j

Jump

Trace.

Jump

Write.

J

j

Write **j** to complete each word.

 ___acket ___og

Help the boy find his kitten.

Match each kitten to its shadow.

5

Trace.

Write.

Write the missing numbers.

1 ___ 3 ___ ___

Count the kittens.
Write how many of each below.

In each set, circle the kitten with **more** toys.

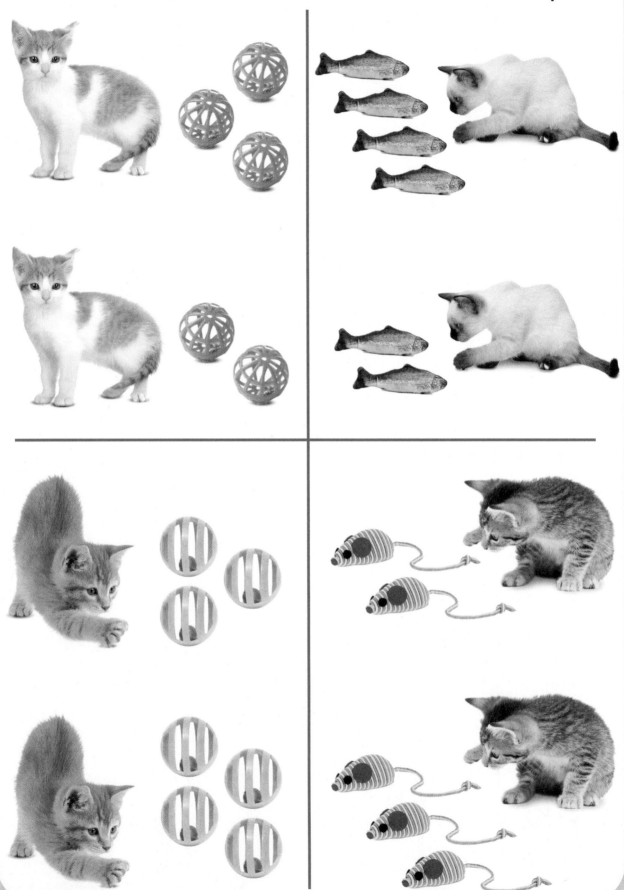

Cut out the pictures below.
Use them to complete each pattern.

Circle 5 differences.

Kk

Kitten

Trace.

Write.

Color the pictures that begin with k.

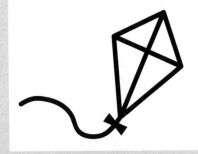

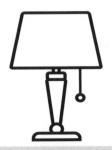

L l

Lick

Trace.

Lick

Write.

L

l

Color the shapes with the letters **L** and **l**.

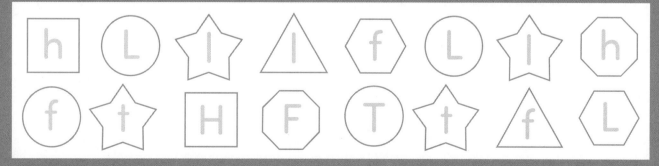

Blue

Circle the things that are blue.

Color the bed 🖍 BLUE 🖍 .

Circle the kitten that is in **front** of the flowers.

Circle the kitten that is **behind** the basketball.

Connect the dots from 1 to 5.
Then color the picture.

Count the kittens. Write the number.

Write the missing letters in each row.

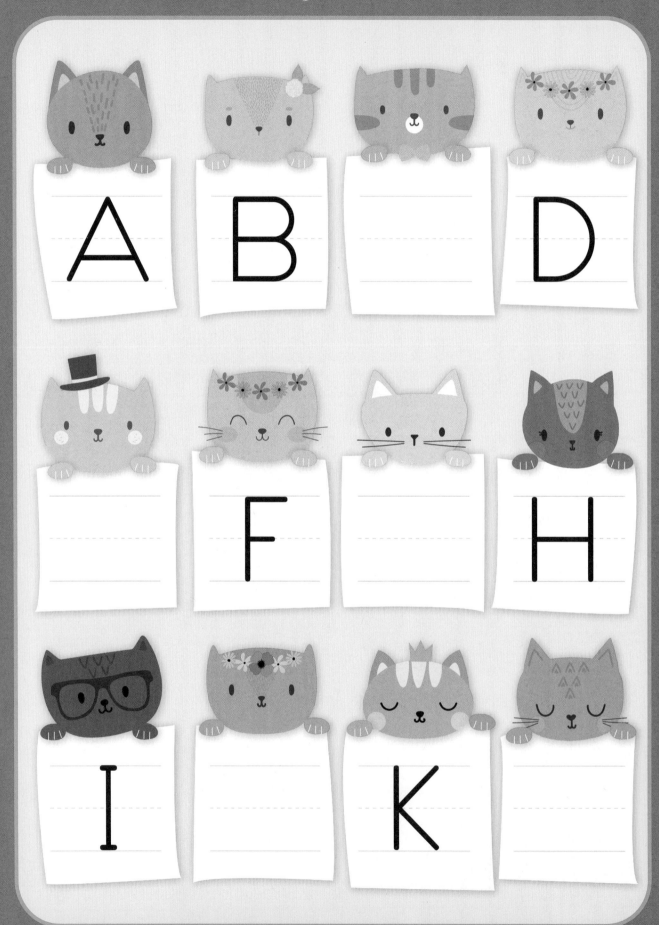

A B _ D

_ F _ H

I _ K _

Cut out the numbers. Paste each next to the set with the same number of kittens.

3 2 5 4

Trace the rectangle and the triangle.

rectangle

triangle

Color the rectangles green. Color the triangles red.

Mm

M Mouse

Trace.

Mouse

Write.

M

m

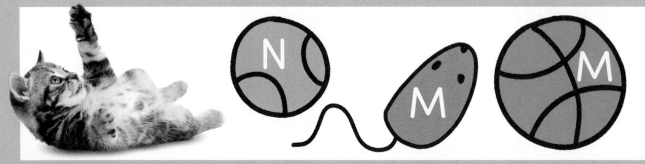

Nn

Nap

Trace.

Write.

Circle **N** and **n**.

M   H   N   h   n   w   M   X
  m   h   W   M   x   H   n
N   X   W   H
  n   W   X   H   x   w   N   w   m   h

Help the children find the kittens.

Count each type of kitten.
Color one box in the graph for each kitten.

© Scholastic Inc.

6

Trace.

Write.

Match each number to a set.

| 4 |
| 6 |
| 5 |

Circle the things that come in **6**'s.

In each set, circle the kitten with **fewer** toys.

Circle **5** differences.

Connect the dots from **A** to **N**.
Then color the picture.

Cut out the uppercase letters. Paste each next to its matching lowercase letter.

e

f

h

m

n

l

E F H M N L

Draw **6** balls for the kittens to play with.

Out

Trace.

Out

Write.

O

o

Color the paw prints with the letters **O** and **o**.

Pp

Play

Trace.

Play

Write.

P

p

Write **p** to complete each word.

 ___uppy  ___ig

Green

Circle the things that are green.

Color the collar 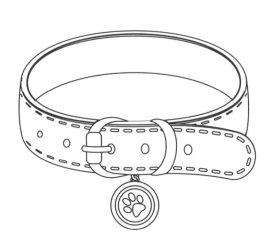.

What comes next? Draw it!

7

7

Trace.

7

Write.

7

Circle each group of **7**.

Find each 7. Color that space YELLOW.
Then color the rest of the picture.

Find and circle these items in the big picture.

Name each picture. What beginning sound does each make? Circle it.

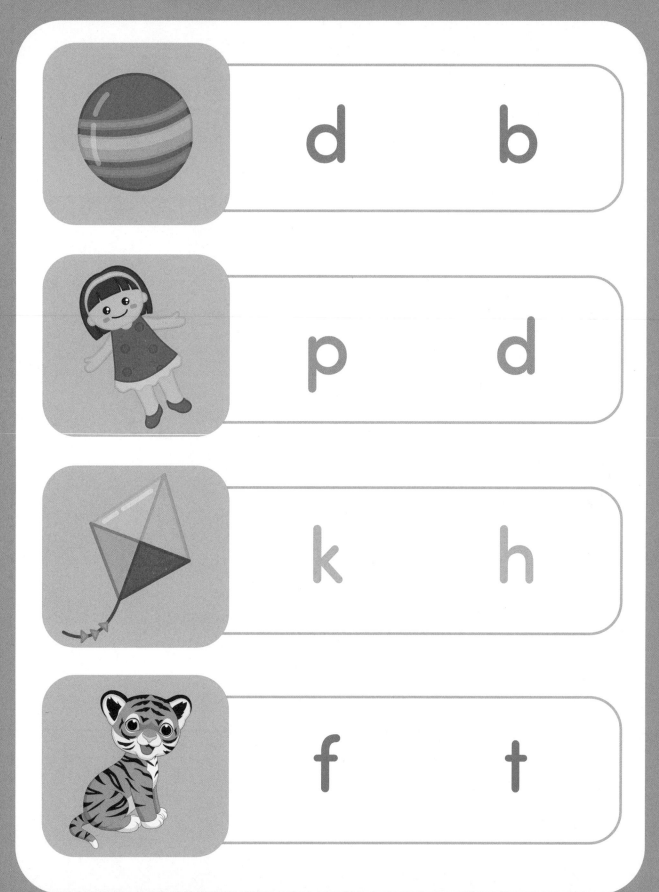

d   b

p   d

k   h

f   t

Qq

Quiet

Trace.

Write.

Write **Q** and **q** on each bed.

Rr

Roar

Trace.

Write.

R

r

Color the pictures that begin with **R**.

Help the kitten find its toy.

Name the parts of a cat.
Then, trace the first letter in each word.

ear

eye

nose

mouth

tail

fur

paw

8

Trace.

8

Write.

Circle each 8.

6   3   6   8   3   3   8   3

3   6   6   3

8   8   6   6   3

3   3   3   8   3   8   6

© Scholastic Inc.

Match each cat to its twin.

Circle the things that come in 8's.

Say each number.
Circle that many kittens in each set.

8

5

7

6

Circle **5** differences.

Cut out the shapes below.
Paste them where they belong in the picture.

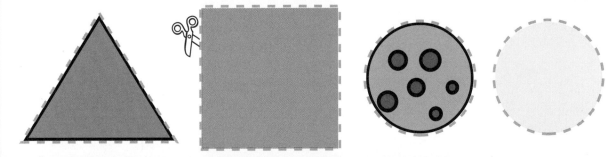

Orange

Circle the things that are orange.

Color the cat  ORANGE.

S s

Scratch

Trace.

Scratch

Write.

S

s

Circle **S** and **s**.

S s q C s c q Q S
c s S Q c Q C
s o c Q o O C
Q O o c Q C O s C Q

T t

Toy

Trace.

Toy

Write.

T

t

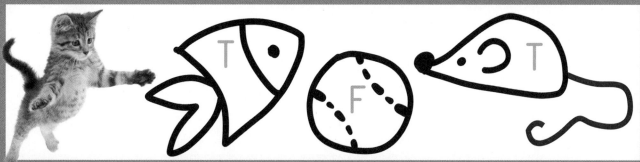

9

Trace.

Write.

9

Color the shapes with the number **9**.

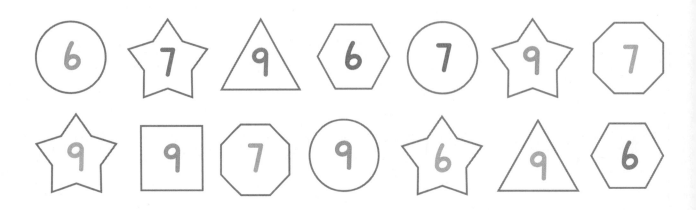

© Scholastic Inc.

Cut out the labels. Paste them next to each part of the kitten.

mouth   eye   tail   paw

tongue   nose   fur   ear

Circle the kitten that is **in** the basket.

Circle the kitten that is **out** of the box.

Count the kittens in each basket.
Circle the number.

7   6   4

1   4   5

5   8   3

9   4   3

What is missing? Cut out the pictures below.
Use them to complete each pattern.

Trace the oval and the diamond.

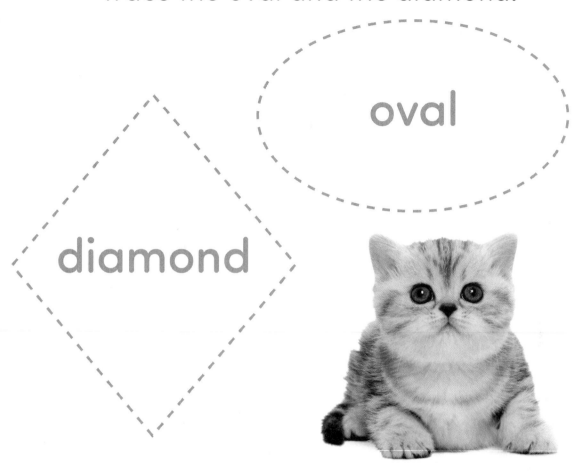

Color the ovals **purple**. Color the diamonds yellow.

Uu

Up

Trace.

Up

Write.

U

u

Color the shapes with the letters **U** and **u**.

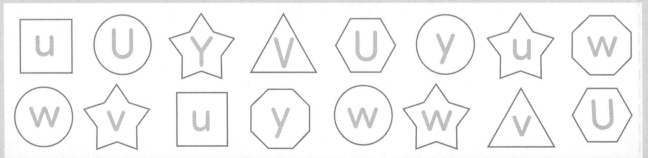

V v

Vet

Trace.

Vet

Write.

V

V

Write **V** and **v** on each bowl.

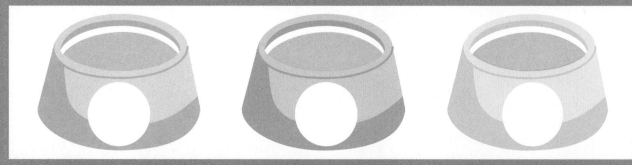

Help the kitten find its friends.

Count each shape.
Color one box in the graph for each shape.

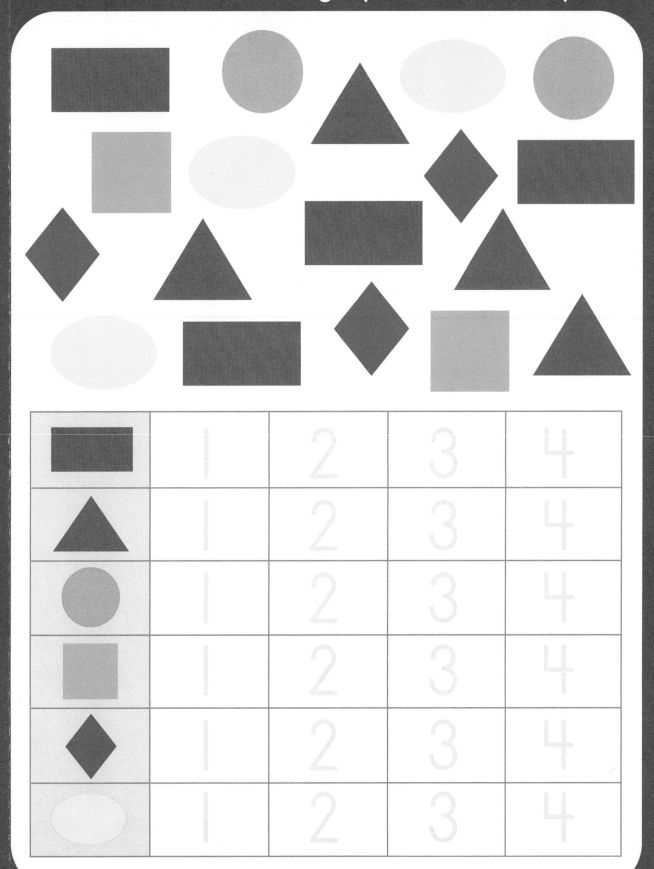

10

Trace.

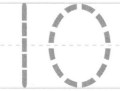

Write.

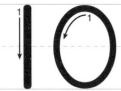

Match each number to a set.

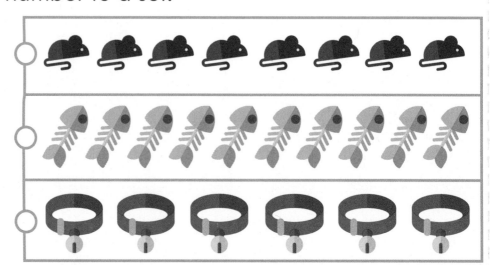

6
8
10

Find and circle 10 in the picture.

Count the cat faces. Write the number.

Cut out the numbers. Paste each next to the set with the same number of fish.

Circle **5** differences.

Ww

Whisker →

Trace.

Whisker

Write.

W

w

Write **W** to complete each word.

___et ___alk

X-ray

Trace.

X-ray

Write.

Circle X and x.

x w K N N n w W X

K n X Y W x K w

X W N x k N Y w W

n

Purple

Circle the things that are purple.

Color the scratch post 🖍 PURPLE.

Draw the missing shape.

Connect the dots from 1 to 10.
Then color the picture.

Color the picture. Use the color key.

Color Key

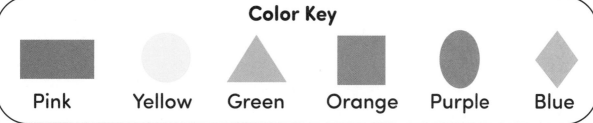

Pink   Yellow   Green   Orange   Purple   Blue

Write the missing letters.

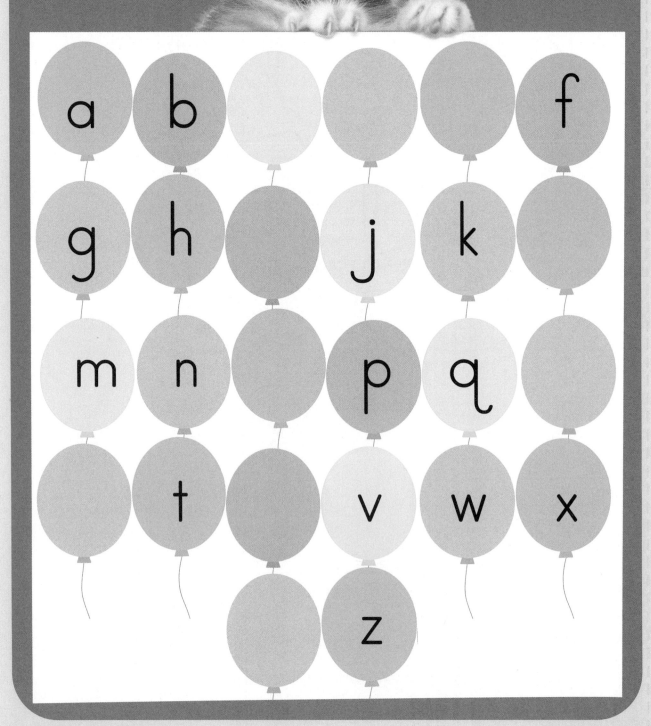

a b ___ ___ ___ f

g h ___ j k ___

m n ___ p q ___

___ t ___ v w x

___ z

Cut out the kittens.
Paste them in the picture.

Find and circle these items in the big picture.

Yum

Trace.

Write.

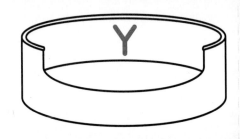

Zz

Zzz

Trace.

Zzz

Write.

Write **Z** on each triangle. Write **z** on each circle.

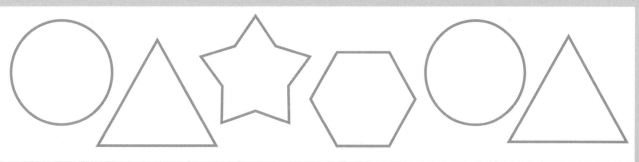

Help the kitten find its mother.

Match each number to a set.

4

2

3

1

In each set, circle the kitten with **more** treats.

Draw 10 spots on the kitten.

Circle the kitten that is **on** the books.

Circle the kitten that is **under** the table.

What letters are missing? Cut out the letters below. Paste each where it belongs.

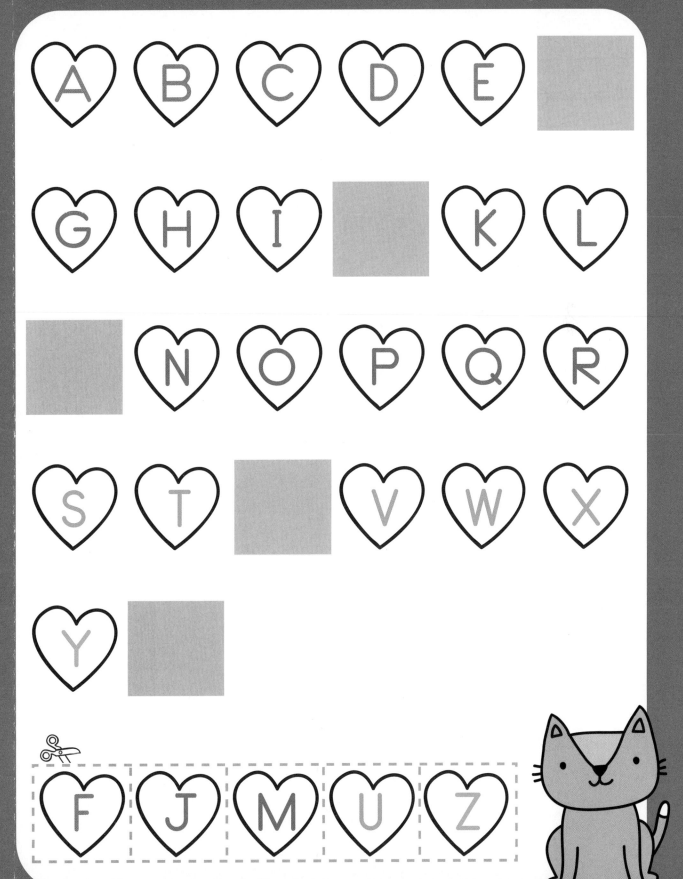

A B C D E ▢

G H I ▢ K L

▢ N O P Q R

S T ▢ V W X

Y ▢

F J M U Z

Connect the dots from **A** to **Z**.
Then color the picture.

Circle **5** differences.

Circle the things that come in **2's**.

Circle **5** differences.

Find and circle these items in the big picture.

Circle **5** differences.

Circle **5** differences.

Circle **5** differences.

Circle **5** differences.

Find and circle these items in the big picture.

CONGRATULATIONS!

This certificate is awarded to

_____

FOR OUTSTANDING ACHIEVEMENT

_____
Signed

_____
Date

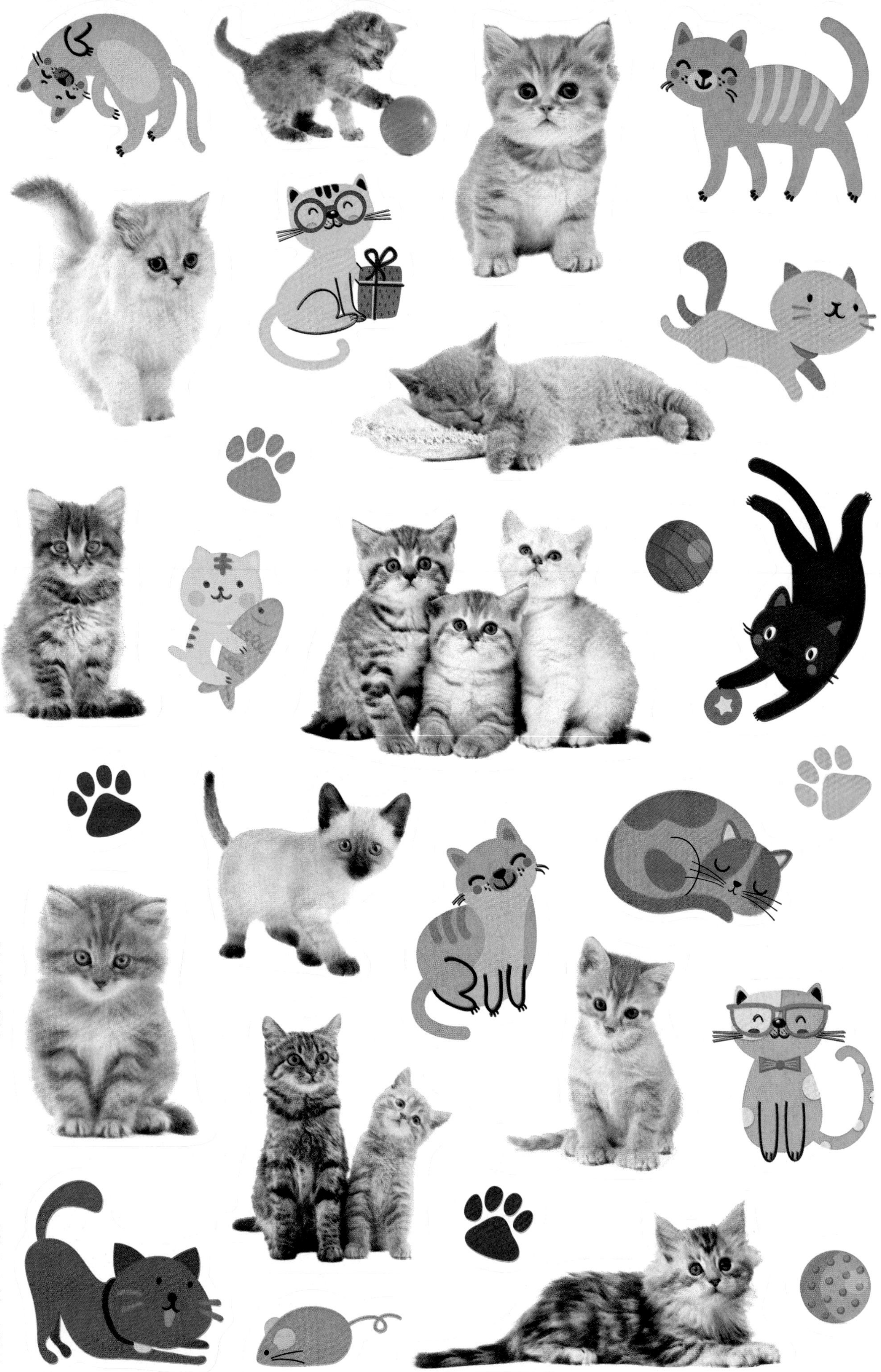

Printed in the U.S.A. PO# 5071464